What Is Me?

Veronica Lane Books

What Is Me?

By Etan Boritzer   Illustrated by Joanna Forbes

Copyright 2025 by Etan Boritzer

All rights reserved. No part of this publication may be reproduced, stored in a retrieval system or transmitted in any form or by any means, electronic, mechanical, photocopying, recording or otherwise without the written permission of the Publisher.

First Printing 2025

Veronica Lane Books
www.VeronicaLaneBooks.com   email: Etan@veronicalanebooks.com
11420 US-1, Ste 124, N. Palm Beach, FL 33408 USA
Tel: +1 (833) VLBOOKS +1 (833-852-6657)

Library of Congress Cataloging-In-Publication Data
    Boritzer, Etan, 1950-
    What Is Me / by Etan Boritzer
    Illustrated by Joanna Forbes -- 1st Edition
    p. cm.

SUMMARY: The author presents various points of view on personal identity.
Audience: Grades K - 6

ISBN 979-89919296-2-2 (Hardbound)
ISBN 979-89919296-3-9 (Paperback)

...to the children of the world...

What is Me?
Me is what you call yourself.
Me is made up of lots of parts.
And there are also different me's.
Sometimes we are not sure who is me,
and who is not me.

How can we ever find out
who is the real me?
Where did me begin
and where will me end?
Maybe there never was a beginning to me
and maybe there will never be an end to me.

Me is a puzzle to me!

What is Me?

When did me begin?
And how did me begin?

From a seed? From a drop of water?
From our cousins, the monkeys?

Who began me?

And why did me even begin?

Was there a me before the beginning of me?
Let's explore me!

Where did me begin?
My birth parents got together
and they made my body.
But where was me before my body was born?

Could there have been a me before my birth?

Maybe there was a me somewhere else,
before this me even showed up here!.
Could that be?

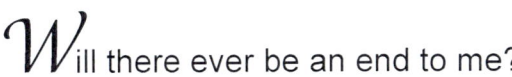

*W*ill there ever be an end to me?

We know that we live in this body
and that all bodies have to stop sometime.
But where does all the stuff inside me go
when the body stops?

Where does all the love inside of me go?

And what about all the feelings
And ideas inside me?
Maybe all that stuff inside me
never stops or ends!

And, if there is never an end
to all the stuff inside of me,
maybe there was also never a beginning
to all the stuff inside me.

What is me really made of?
Well, the outside me is called my body—
my face, my skin, my arms and legs,
my eyes and ears—
and everything else that you can see of me.

Sometimes kids like the outside me,
but sometimes they don't.

Sometimes kids don't like me
because of my skin color,
or because of my clothes,
or because of my talk,
or because my body needs a wheelchair.
Sometimes kids think they know me
because of that outside stuff of me
that they can see.

Well, all that outside stuff is just part of me—
not *all* of me.

*W*hat is inside me?

Inside me are muscles and bones,
my heart pumping blood,
my stomach digesting food,
and my lungs filling in and out with air.

There are also billions of little cells
everywhere inside me
that do all kinds of different jobs.
There is some pee
and some poop inside me too.

And inside my head,
there is a big, powerful brain!

And inside my brain is my beautiful mind!

Everybody can see the outside me,
and a doctor can see the inside me,
but nobody but me can really see
what's inside my beautiful mind.

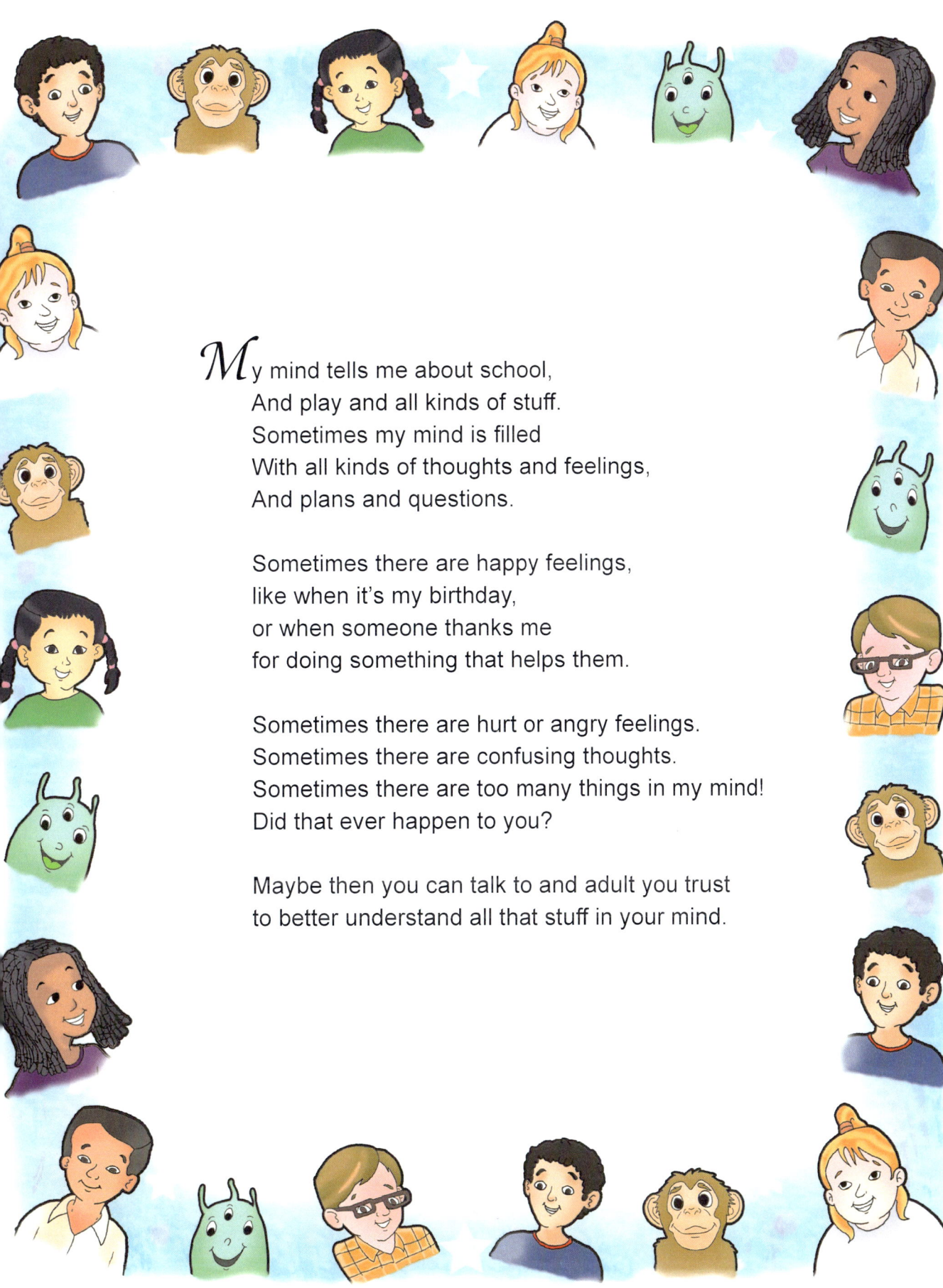

My mind tells me about school,
And play and all kinds of stuff.
Sometimes my mind is filled
With all kinds of thoughts and feelings,
And plans and questions.

Sometimes there are happy feelings,
like when it's my birthday,
or when someone thanks me
for doing something that helps them.

Sometimes there are hurt or angry feelings.
Sometimes there are confusing thoughts.
Sometimes there are too many things in my mind!
Did that ever happen to you?

Maybe then you can talk to and adult you trust
to better understand all that stuff in your mind.

*I*f there is too much stuff in my mind,
or too much stuff outside my mind,
(or too much stuff inside my body,
or even on my body),
meditation can help me.

Meditation is when we sit quietly
and watch our breath go in and out.
Have you tried meditation?
It really helps you feel calm inside.

Even going to a nice park
with my family or friends,
and breathing some nice clean air,
and noticing a weird bug on a flower,
helps to let go of stuff that is bothering me.

There are *soooo* many interesting things
going on inside my mind!

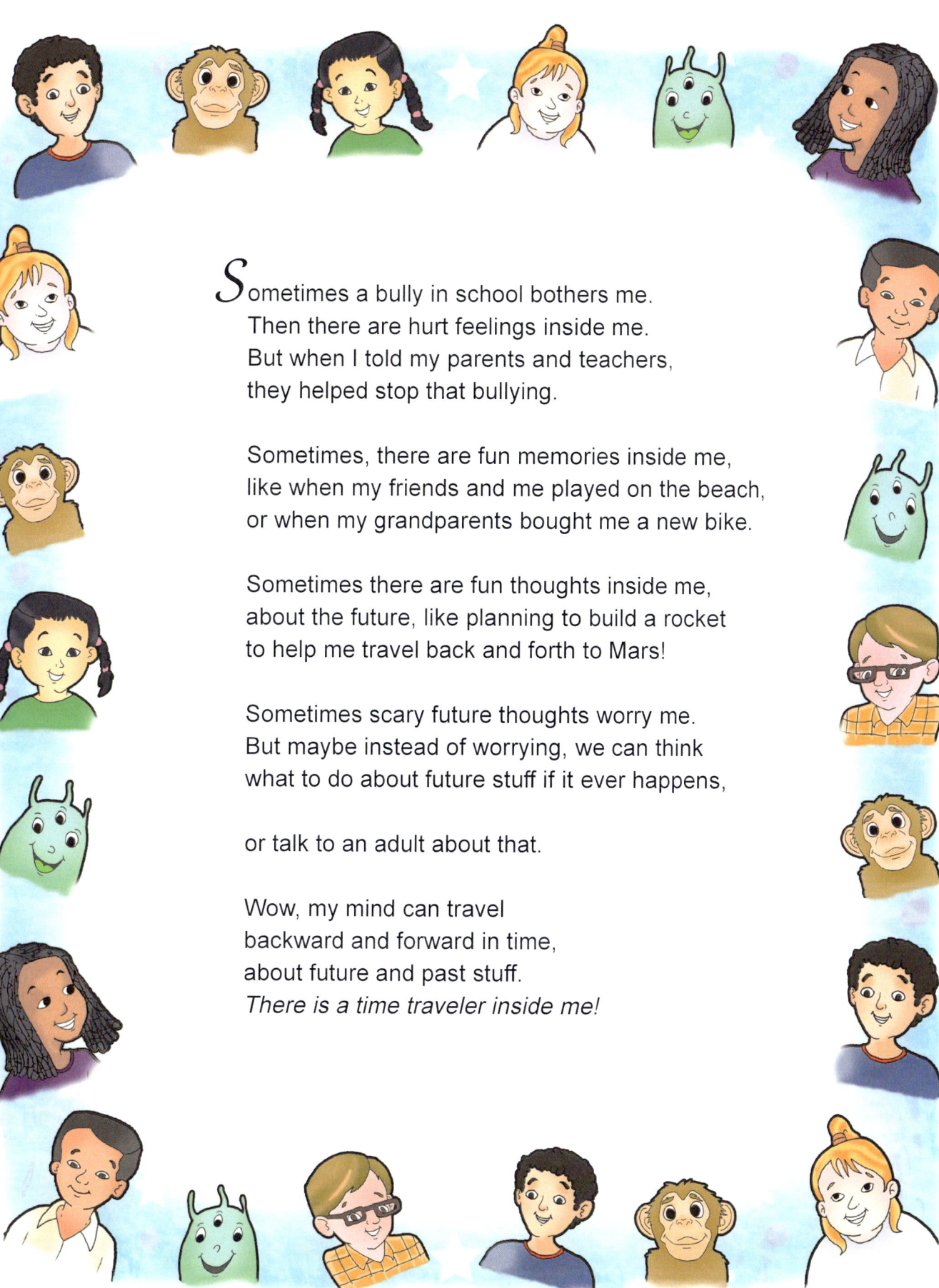

Sometimes a bully in school bothers me.
Then there are hurt feelings inside me.
But when I told my parents and teachers,
they helped stop that bullying.

Sometimes, there are fun memories inside me,
like when my friends and me played on the beach,
or when my grandparents bought me a new bike.

Sometimes there are fun thoughts inside me,
about the future, like planning to build a rocket
to help me travel back and forth to Mars!

Sometimes scary future thoughts worry me.
But maybe instead of worrying, we can think
what to do about future stuff if it ever happens,

or talk to an adult about that.

Wow, my mind can travel
backward and forward in time,
about future and past stuff.
There is a time traveler inside me!

What else is inside me?
Hmmm, it's hard to explain but sometimes
there is a feeling of something really big
inside me called Wonder!

Like when we went to see the Grand Canyon.
It was so big and awesome, and wonderful!
This same wonder happens to me at night,
looking up at the billions of stars
shining and blinking in the dark night sky.

What is wonder?
And why does it happen inside me?
Did you ever experience wonder?

There is also character inside me.
Character is part of my deepest self,
the part is honest and fair, respectful and caring.
People say we have good character,
if we say or do something nice for somebody
who is hurt or unhappy.

Even if we think healing thoughts
for somebody who is sick or unhappy,
or if we do little things for others,
like being kind and caring,
that is part of our character.

The character inside me is always growing.
This part of me gets better and better
as life teaches me new lessons.

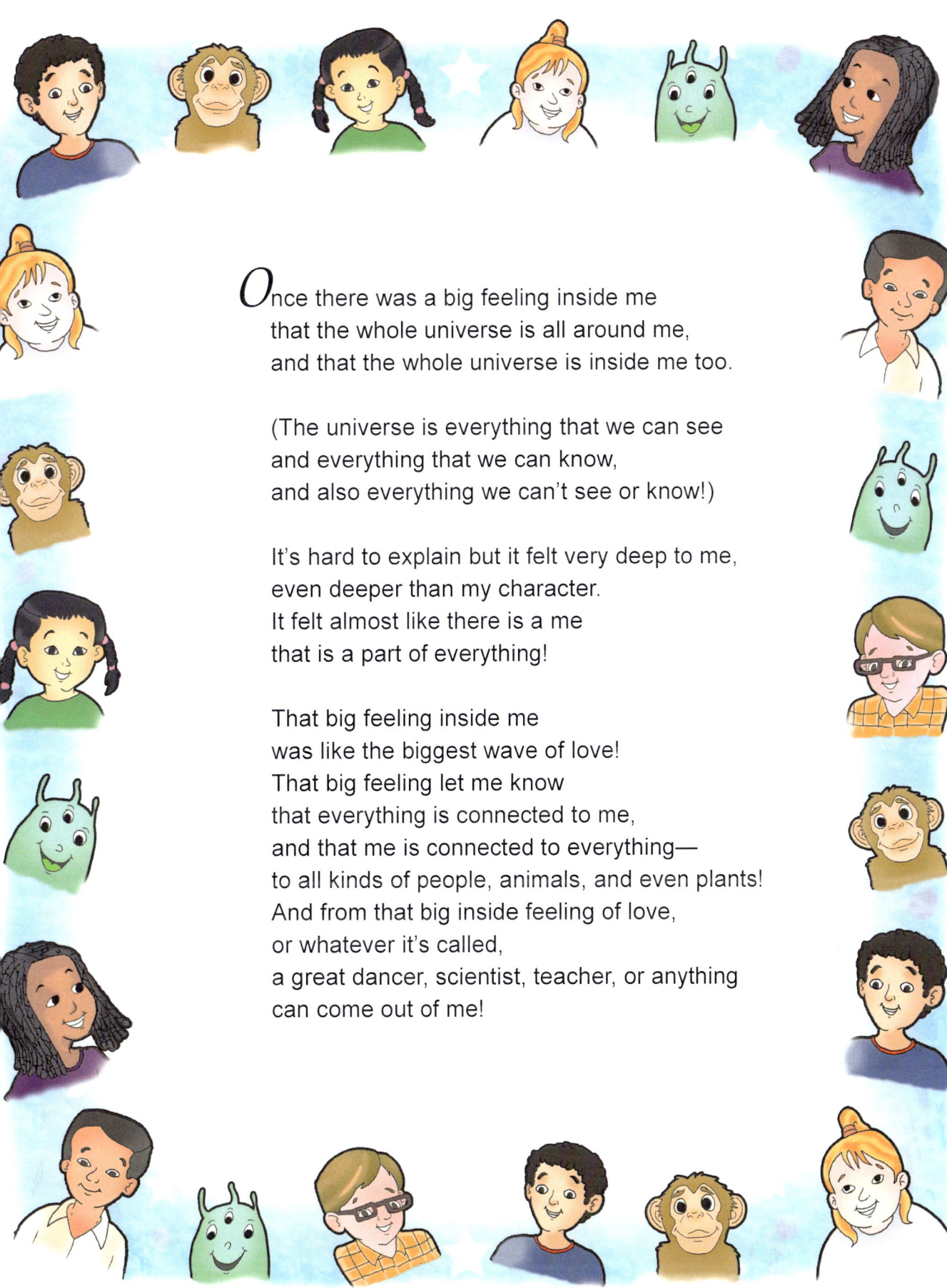

*O*nce there was a big feeling inside me
that the whole universe is all around me,
and that the whole universe is inside me too.

(The universe is everything that we can see
and everything that we can know,
and also everything we can't see or know!)

It's hard to explain but it felt very deep to me,
even deeper than my character.
It felt almost like there is a me
that is a part of everything!

That big feeling inside me
was like the biggest wave of love!
That big feeling let me know
that everything is connected to me,
and that me is connected to everything—
to all kinds of people, animals, and even plants!
And from that big inside feeling of love,
or whatever it's called,
a great dancer, scientist, teacher, or anything
can come out of me!

*D*id you ever feel that big inside feeling?
Like you are connected to everything,
and everything is connected to you?

Can anyone feel that feeling?

Maybe if we get really quiet for a minute,
just breathing, and really listening —
just completely quiet,
maybe we can all feel that big inside feeling
that connects us to everything.

Then, maybe we can also feel
that everything around us is smiling at us,
and that we live in a big and friendly universe.

Shhhhhhh....

Can you feel it?

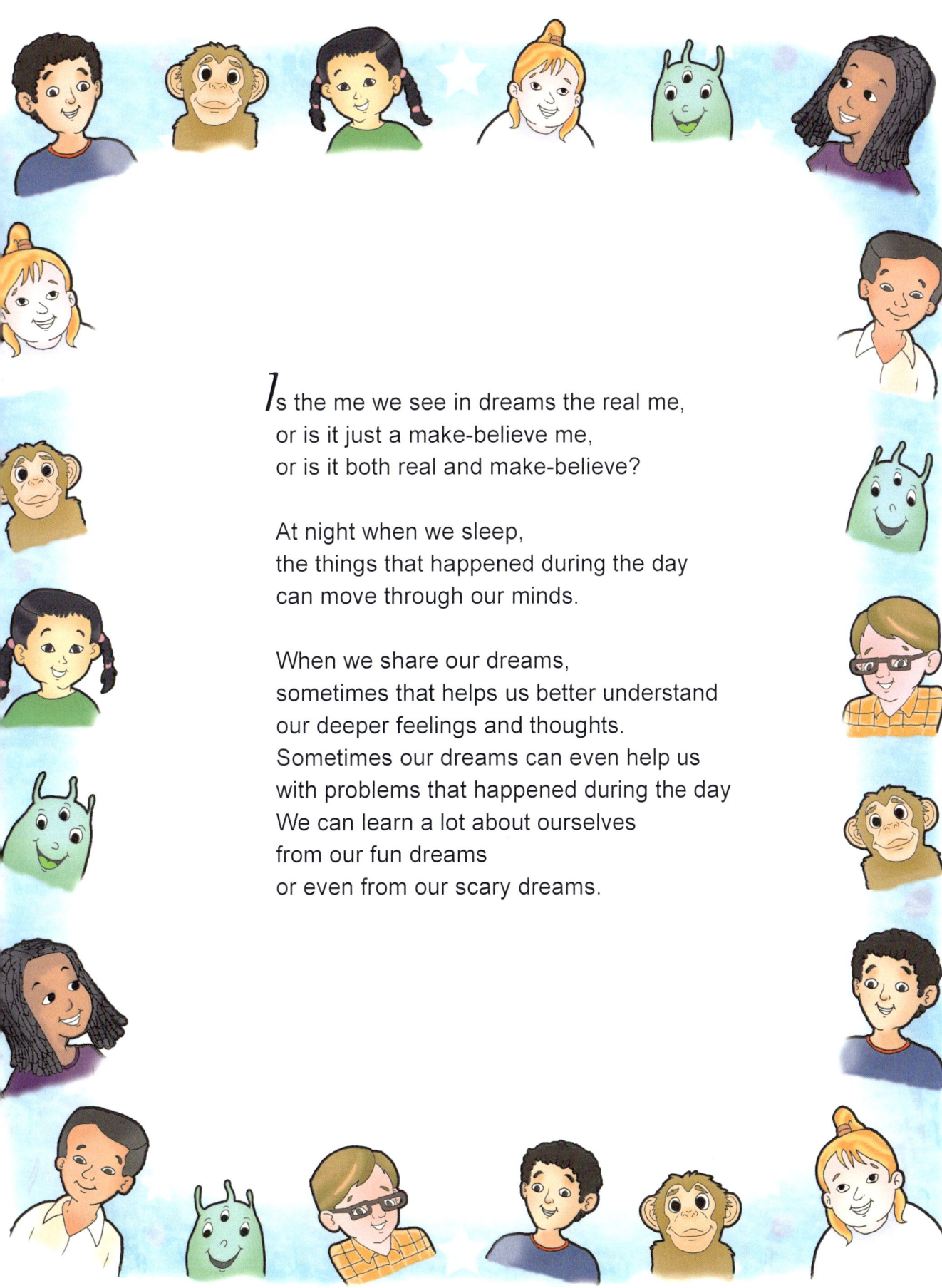

Is the me we see in dreams the real me,
or is it just a make-believe me,
or is it both real and make-believe?

At night when we sleep,
the things that happened during the day
can move through our minds.

When we share our dreams,
sometimes that helps us better understand
our deeper feelings and thoughts.
Sometimes our dreams can even help us
with problems that happened during the day
We can learn a lot about ourselves
from our fun dreams
or even from our scary dreams.

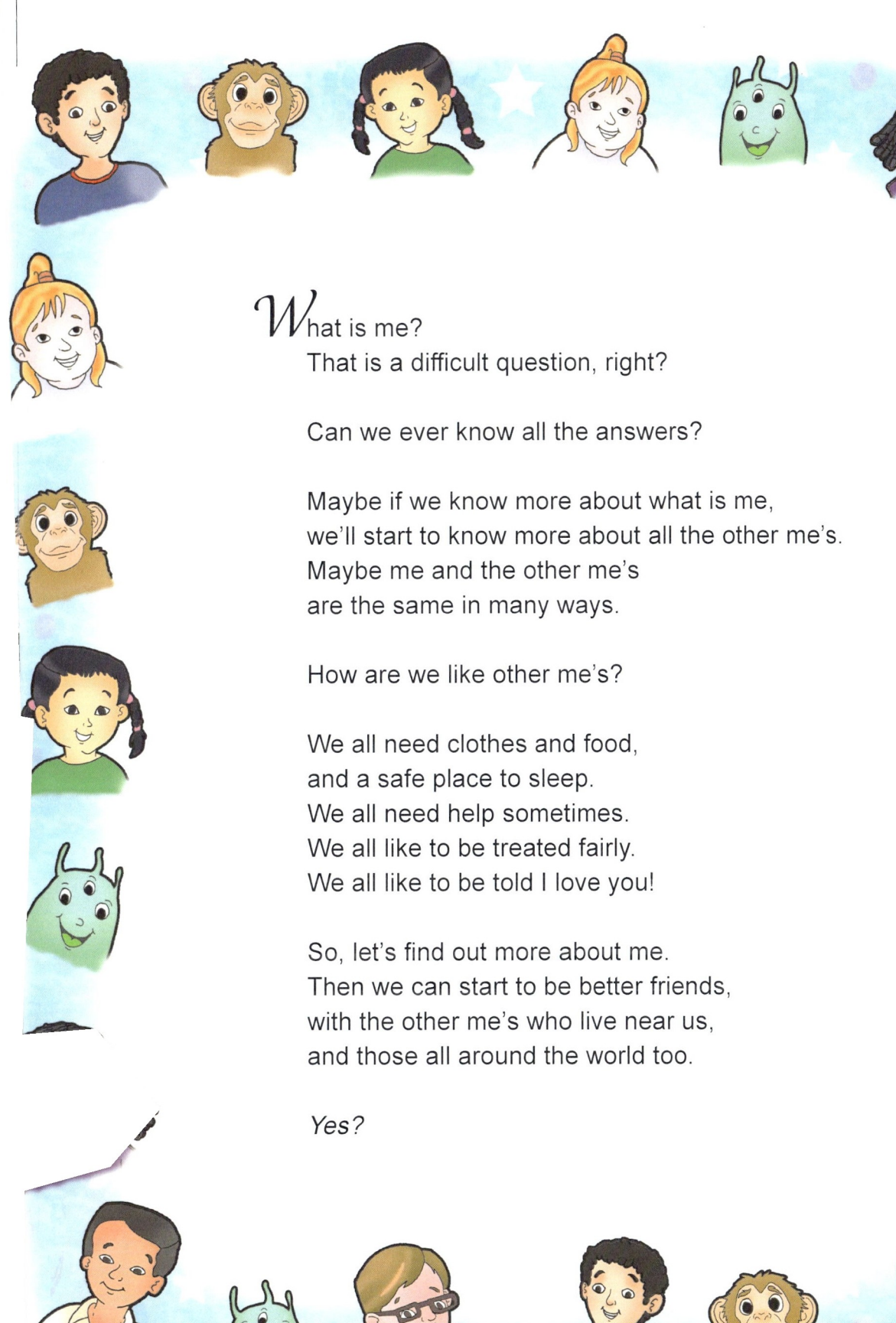

What is me?
That is a difficult question, right?

Can we ever know all the answers?

Maybe if we know more about what is me,
we'll start to know more about all the other me's.
Maybe me and the other me's
are the same in many ways.

How are we like other me's?

We all need clothes and food,
and a safe place to sleep.
We all need help sometimes.
We all like to be treated fairly.
We all like to be told I love you!

So, let's find out more about me.
Then we can start to be better friends,
with the other me's who live near us,
and those all around the world too.

Yes?

*I*sn't it fun to think about what is me?

Each of us could write their own book
on the subject of what is me, right?

What does me want, or not want?
What feels good to me?
What doesn't feel good to me?

What about my thoughts and feelings?
What should we do with all of them?

What friends are good for me?
What friends are not good for me?

What about my nighttime dreams?
All kinds of fun, and sometimes scary things
happen to me in my dreams.

www.ingramcontent.com/pod-product-compliance
Lightning Source LLC
LaVergne TN
LVRC090726070526
838199LV00019B/545